¿Qué hace el ESPECIALISTA DE MEDIOS DE LA BIBLIOTECA ESCOLAR?

What Does a LIBRARY MEDIA SPECIALIST Do?

Winston Garrett

Traducido por Eida de la Vega

PowerKiDS press

Published in 2015 by The Rosen Publishing Group, Inc.
29 East 21st Street, New York, NY 10010

First Edition

Editor: Norman D. Graubart
Book Design: Colleen Bialecki
Photo Research: Katie Stryker

Spanish Translation: Eida de la Vega

Photo Credits: Cover Kathy Dewar/E+/Getty Images; p. 5 Cynthia Farmer/Shutterstock.com; p. 6 Shalom Ormsby/Blend Images/Getty Images; p. 9 Looking Glass/Blend Images/Getty Images; p. 10 Ryan McGinnis/Flickr/Getty Images; p. 13 andresrimaging/iStock/Thinkstock; p. 14 Digital Vision/Photodisc/Getty Images; p. 17 Blend Images/Shutterstock.com; p. 18 wavebreakmedia/Shutterstock.com; p. 21 Ingram Publishing/Thinkstock; p. 22 Courtesy of The Historical Society of Glastonbury, Connecticut.

Publisher's Cataloging Data

Garrett, Winston.
What does a library media specialist do? = ¿Qué hace el especialista de medios de la biblioteca escolar? / by Winston Garrett, translated by Eida de la Vega — first edition.
p. cm. — (Jobs in my school = Oficios en mi escuela)
Parallel title: Oficios en mi escuela
In English and Spanish.
Includes index.
ISBN 978-1-4777-6796-2 (library binding)
1. School libraries — United States — Juvenile literature. 2. School librarians — United States — Juvenile literature. I. Title.
Z675.S3 W56 2015
027.8—d23

Websites: Due to the changing nature of Internet links, PowerKids Press has developed an online list of websites related to the subject of this book. This site is updated regularly. Please use this link to access the list: www.powerkidslinks.com/josc/libr/

Manufactured in the United States of America

CPSIA Compliance Information: Batch #WS14PK4: For Further Information contact Rosen Publishing, New York, New York at 1-800-237-9932

CONTENIDO

Acerca de las bibliotecas 4
En la biblioteca 12
Historia de la biblioteca 23
Palabras que debes saber 24
Índice 24

CONTENTS

About Libraries 4
In the Library 12
Library History 23
Words to Know 24
Index 24

La gente pide prestados libros en la **biblioteca**.

People borrow books at the **library**.

LIBRARY

¡Pedir libros prestados es gratis!

Borrowing books is free!

Hay un **plazo** para devolver los libros.

Books are due on the **due date**.

DATE DUE

The Library charges fines on overdues.

OCT 1 2 1994 NOV 2 1994

NOV 2 1994 NOV 2 3 1994

NOV 1 3 1996 DEC 0 4 1996

RETURNED

NOVEX OCT 3 0 2001

RETURNED

MAR 3 1 2005

RETURNED

RETURNED

RETURNED

JAN 30 2012

#1901

La biblioteca más grande de los Estados Unidos es la Biblioteca del Congreso.

America's biggest library is the Library of Congress.

Los especialistas de medios trabajan en la biblioteca.

Library media specialists run the library.

DELUXE
UNABRIDGED
DICTIONARY

Leen cuentos a los niños.

They read stories to the children.

¡Ayudan mucho!

They are helpful!

Children's
New

También se les llama bibliotecarios.

They are also called librarians.

Usan el **Sistema Decimal Dewey** para clasificar los libros. Este sistema lo creó Melvil Dewey.

They use the **Dewey Decimal System** to sort books. Melvil Dewey came up with it.

649.5
P2287p
2006

Mary Kingsbury fue la primera bibliotecaria escolar titulada.

Mary Kingsbury was the first trained school librarian.

PALABRAS QUE DEBES SABER
WORDS TO KNOW

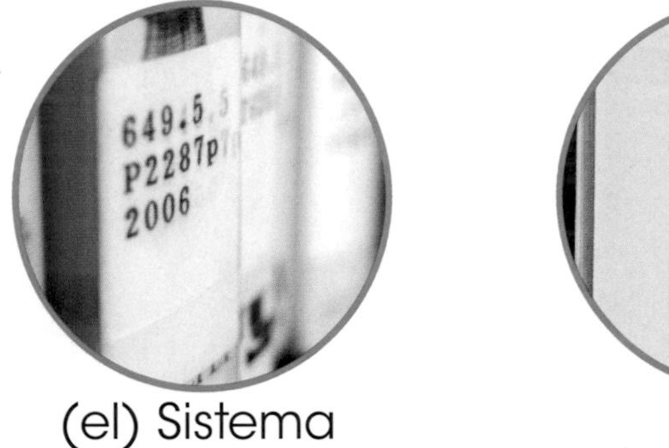

(el) Sistema Decimal Dewey

Dewey Decimal System

(los) plazos

due dates

(la) biblioteca

library

ÍNDICE

B
biblioteca, 4, 11–12
bibliotecaria/o(s), 19, 23

G
gente, 4

L
lectura, 15
libros, 4, 7-8, 20

INDEX

B
books, 4, 7–8, 20

L
librarian(s), 19, 23
library, 4, 11–12

P
people, 4

R
reading, 15